Yellow Umbrella Books are published by Capstone Press
151 Good Counsel Drive, P.O. Box 669, Mankato, Minnesota 56002
http://www.capstone-press.com

Library of Congress Cataloging-in-Publication Data
Tucker, Shirley.
   Looking at shapes/by Shirley Tucker and Jane Rambo
   p. cm. —(Math)
   Includes Index.
   Summary: Photographs and simple text describe examples of such shapes as rectangles, squares, triangles, and circles.
   ISBN 0-7368-1284-9 (hardcover)
   1. Geometry—Juvenile literature. [1. Shape.] I. Title. II. Series.
QA445.5 .T83 2002
516—dc21   2002016832

Editorial Credits
Susan Evento, Managing Editor/Product Development; Elizabeth Jaffe, Senior Editor; Sydney Wright and Charles Hunt, Designers; Kimberly Danger and Heidi Schoof, Photo Rsearchers
Photo Credits
Cover: Michael Manheim/Photo Network; Title Page: Richard Cummins; Page 2: Jim Schwabel/Photo Network; Page 3: Leslie O'Shaughnessy (top), Richard Cummins (bottom); Page 4: Photri-Microstock (top and bottom); Page 5: Index Stock (top), Henry T. Kaiser/Photo Network; Page 6: Jack Glisson; Page 7: K.H. Photo/International Stock (top), Jack Glisson (bottom); Page 8: J.G. Faircloth/Transparencies, Inc. (top), Photri-Microstock (bottom); Page 9: Leslie O'Shaughnessy (top), Ingrid Marn Wood & Claire Hall (bottom); Page 10: Leslie O'Shaughnessy, Page 11: Photri-Microstock (left), Dario Perla/International Stock (right); Page 12: Miwako Ikeda/International Stock (top left), Leslie O'Shaughnessy (top right), Sylvan Wittwer/Visuals Unlimited (bottom); Page 13: Grace Davies/Photo Network, Page 14: Morris Best/Uniphoto (left), Johnny Stockshooter/International Stock, Page 15: Index Stock (top left), Uniphoto (top right), Chad Ehlers/International Stock (bottom), Page 16: James L. Shaffer

Looking at Shapes

By Dr. Shirley Tucker and
Jane Rambo

Consulting Editor: Gail Saunders-Smith, Ph.D.
Consultants: Claudine Jellison and Patricia Williams,
Reading Recovery Teachers
Content Consultant: Johanna Kaufman,
Math Learning/Resource Director of the Dalton School

Yellow Umbrella Books
an imprint of Capstone Press
Mankato, Minnesota

This door is a rectangle.
It has four sides.
Its opposite sides
are the same size.

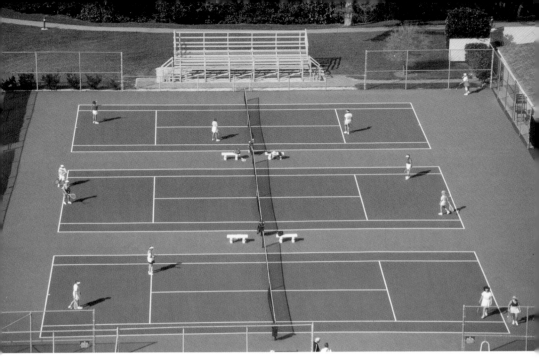

We see rectangles all around us. They are different sizes. But they are all the same shape.

This sign is a rectangle.

This pool is a rectangle.

A football field is a rectangle.

This flag is a rectangle too.

This stamp is a square.
It has four sides.
Its sides are the same size.
Its four corners
are all the same size.

We see squares all around us.
They are different sizes.
But they are all the same shape.

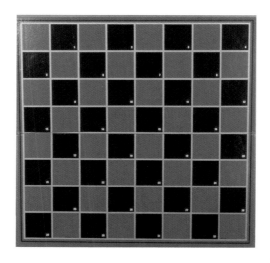

This base is a square.

The boxes on this calendar are squares.

SUNDAY	MONDAY	TUESDAY	WEDNESDAY	THURSDAY	FRIDAY	SATURDAY
AUGUST	OCTOBER	1	2	3	4	5
6 Full Moon	7 Labor Day	8	9	10	11	12
13 Last Quarter Grandparent's Day	14	15	16	17	18	19
20 New Moon	21 Rosh Hashana	22	23	24	25	26
27	28 First Quarter	29	30 Yom Kippur	**September**		

Keys on a keyboard
are squares.

The windows on this house
are squares too.

This sail is a triangle.
It has three sides.
Its sides can be
different sizes.
It has three corners.
Its corners can be
different sizes too.

We see triangles
all around us.
They are different sizes.

Roofs of houses
can be triangles.
The eyes and nose of this
jack-o'-lantern are triangles.
The sides of pyramids
are triangles too.

These cookies are circles.
Circles are round.
They do not have corners.

We see circles all around us.
They are different sizes.
But they are all the same shape.

A tire is a circle.

A Ferris wheel is a circle.

The middle of this sunflower
is a circle too.

What shapes do you see?

Words to Know/Index

Word Count: 235
Early-Intervention Level: 10